MICHELE SCICOLONE

Risotto

Photography by SIMON WHEELER

THE MASTER CHEFS

WEIDENFELD & NICOLSON

LONDON

MICHELE SCICOLONE is a writer who specializes in food, wine and travel. Her latest book, *La Dolce Vita*, is a collection of recipes for 'life's sweet pleasures', Italian desserts. It was nominated as Best Dessert Book of 1994 by the International Association of Cooking Professionals. Her previous book, *The Antipasto Table*, was nominated as Best Italian Cookbook of 1991 by the James Beard Foundation. Michele is also the author of two books on fish cookery.

Michele writes for *The New York Times*, *Gourmet*, *Food & Wine* and *Eating Well* magazines and is a contributing editor to *Wine Enthusiast* magazine and the *Berlitz Travellers' Guide to Northern Italy*. She teaches cooking at schools around the United States and has appeared on national television on *CBS Morning Show*, *Good Morning America* and *The Home Show* as well as many local television and radio programmes.

CONTENTS

At the table one

is always happy.

ITALIAN PROVERB

INTRODUCTION

There are as many ways to make risotto as there are cooks in
Italy – I have never tasted one that was properly made that I
did not like. Since risotto needs to be prepared at the last
minute, restaurants usually do not make it well. It is, however,
a dish that a home cook can produce superbly.

One of the best things about risotto is that it can be made
with practically any kind of flavouring ingredients: vegetables,
meat, seafood, cheese and even fruit.

The recipes in this collection are some of my favourite
risottos, gathered throughout northern Italy. I have chosen
them because they reflect a wide diversity of ingredients.
I hope they will inspire you to experiment, using the
techniques outlined here to develop your own combinations
of flavours.

Michele Sindona

TOMATO AND BASIL RISOTTO

1.5 LITRES/2½ PINTS CHICKEN
STOCK (PAGE 30)
3 TABLESPOONS UNSALTED BUTTER
1 TABLESPOON OLIVE OIL
2–3 SHALLOTS OR 1 ONION, FINELY
CHOPPED
400 G/14 OZ MEDIUM-GRAIN RICE
125 ML/4 FL OZ DRY WHITE WINE
450 G/1 LB FRESH TOMATOES,
SEEDED AND CHOPPED, OR
400 G/14 OZ CANNED
TOMATOES, PASSED THROUGH A
FOOD MILL
SALT AND FRESHLY GROUND BLACK
PEPPER
LARGE BUNCH OF BASIL, CHOPPED
50 G/2 OZ PARMESAN CHEESE,
GRATED

SERVES 4–6

Heat the stock to just below simmering point.

In a large saucepan, melt 2 tablespoons of the butter with the oil over medium heat. Add the shallots or onion and cook until tender, about 3 minutes.

Add the rice and stir for 2 minutes, until it is coated with the butter. Add the wine and continue to cook and stir until the liquid is absorbed. Add the tomatoes and cook for 1 minute.

Add the hot stock, 125 ml/ 4 fl oz at a time, stirring constantly and making sure the liquid has been absorbed before adding more. After about 10 minutes, stir in salt and pepper to taste. If more liquid is required, use hot water. The risotto is done when the rice grains are tender, yet still firm to the bite.

Remove the pan from the heat and stir in the remaining butter, the basil and the Parmesan cheese. Serve at once.

LEEK AND PANCETTA RISOTTO

2 LEEKS
1.5 LITRES/2½ PINTS CHICKEN
    STOCK (PAGE 30)
2 TABLESPOONS UNSALTED BUTTER
1 TABLESPOON OLIVE OIL
50 G/2 OZ CHOPPED PANCETTA OR
    BLANCHED BACON
400 G/14 OZ MEDIUM-GRAIN RICE
125 ML/4 FL OZ DRY WHITE WINE
SALT AND FRESHLY GROUND BLACK
    PEPPER
50 G/2 OZ PARMESAN CHEESE,
    GRATED

SERVES 4–6

Trim the leeks and cut them in half lengthways. Rinse well, then cut into thin slices.

Heat the stock to just below simmering point.

In a large saucepan, melt the butter with the oil over medium heat. Add the pancetta or bacon and cook until lightly browned, about 5 minutes. Add the leeks and cook until tender, about 5 minutes.

Add the rice and stir for 2 minutes, until it is coated with the butter. Add the wine and stir until the liquid is absorbed.

Add the hot stock, 125 ml/ 4 fl oz at a time, stirring constantly and making sure the liquid has been absorbed before adding more. After about 10 minutes, stir in salt and pepper to taste. If more liquid is required, use hot water. The risotto is done when the rice grains are tender, yet still firm to the bite.

Remove the pan from the heat and stir in the Parmesan cheese. Serve at once.

ITALIAN SAUSAGE RISOTTO
with mushrooms

1.5 LITRES/2½ PINTS MEAT STOCK
(PAGE 30)

2 TABLESPOONS UNSALTED BUTTER

1 TABLESPOON OLIVE OIL

1 ONION, FINELY CHOPPED

225 G/8 OZ ITALIAN SAUSAGES,
CASINGS REMOVED

225 G/8 OZ MUSHROOMS, SLICED

400 G/14 OZ MEDIUM-GRAIN RICE

125 ML/4 FL OZ DRY WHITE WINE

SALT AND FRESHLY GROUND BLACK
PEPPER

50 G/2 OZ PARMESAN CHEESE,
GRATED

SERVES 4–6

Heat the stock to just below simmering point.

In a large saucepan, melt the butter with the oil over medium heat. Add the onion and cook until tender, about 5 minutes.

Add the sausages and cook, stirring frequently to break up the lumps. When the sausages are lightly browned, add the mushrooms and cook for 2 minutes or until just wilted.

Add the rice and stir for 2 minutes, until it is coated with the butter. Add the wine and stir until the liquid is absorbed.

Add the hot stock, 125 ml/ 4 fl oz at a time, stirring constantly and making sure the liquid has been absorbed before adding more. After about 10 minutes, stir in salt and pepper to taste. If more liquid is required, use hot water. The risotto is done when the rice grains are tender, yet still firm to the bite.

Remove the pan from the heat and stir in the Parmesan cheese. Serve at once.

ROASTED BEETROOT RISOTTO

4 BEETROOT, TRIMMED

1.5 LITRES/2½ PINTS CHICKEN
  STOCK (PAGE 30)

3 TABLESPOONS UNSALTED BUTTER

1 TABLESPOON OLIVE OIL

1 ONION, FINELY CHOPPED

400 G/14 OZ MEDIUM-GRAIN RICE

175 ML/6 FL OZ DRY WHITE WINE

SALT AND FRESHLY GROUND BLACK
  PEPPER

50 G/2 OZ PARMESAN CHEESE,
  GRATED

SERVES 4–6

Preheat the oven to 230°C/450°F/ Gas Mark 8. Place the beetroot on a sheet of foil and bake in the preheated oven for 45–60 minutes or until tender when pierced with a knife. Leave to cool. Peel off the skins and chop the beetroot.

For the risotto, heat the stock to just below simmering point.

In a large saucepan, melt 2 tablespoons of the butter with the oil over medium heat. Add the onion and cook until tender.

Add the rice and stir for 2 minutes. Add the wine and continue to cook and stir until the liquid is absorbed. Add the beetroot and cook for 1 minute.

Add the hot stock, 125 ml/4 fl oz at a time, stirring constantly and making sure the liquid has been absorbed before adding more. After about 10 minutes, stir in salt and pepper to taste. If more liquid is required, use hot water. The risotto is done when the rice grains are tender, yet still firm to the bite.

Remove the pan from the heat and stir in the remaining butter and the cheese. Serve at once.

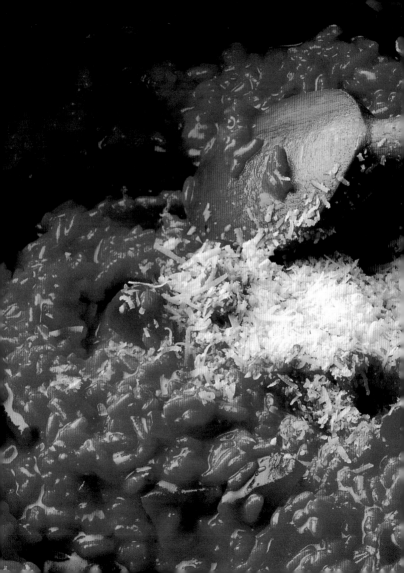

RED WINE RISOTTO

1.5 LITRES/2½ PINTS MEAT STOCK
   (PAGE 30)
3 TABLESPOONS UNSALTED BUTTER
1 TABLESPOON OLIVE OIL
1 ONION, FINELY CHOPPED
1 LARGE GARLIC CLOVE, FINELY
   CHOPPED
400 G/14 OZ MEDIUM-GRAIN RICE
2 TEASPOONS TOMATO PURÉE
250 ML/8 FL OZ DRY RED WINE,
   SUCH AS BARBERA
SALT AND FRESHLY GROUND BLACK
   PEPPER
50 G/2 OZ PARMESAN CHEESE,
   GRATED

SERVES 4–6

Heat the stock to just below simmering point.

In a large saucepan, melt 2 tablespoons of the butter with the oil over medium heat. Add the onion and cook until tender, about 5 minutes. Add the garlic and cook for a further 1 minute.

Add the rice and stir for 2 minutes, until it is heated and coated with the butter.

Mix the tomato purée with 125 ml/4 fl oz of the stock. Add to the rice and stir until the liquid is completely absorbed. Add the wine and continue to cook, stirring, until the liquid is absorbed.

Add the remaining hot stock, 125 ml/4 fl oz at a time, stirring constantly and making sure the liquid has been absorbed before adding more. After about 10 minutes, stir in salt and pepper to taste. If more liquid is required, use hot water. The risotto is done when the rice grains are tender, yet still firm to the bite.

Remove the pan from the heat and stir in the remaining butter and the cheese. Serve at once.

PRAWN AND SCALLOP RISOTTO

3 TABLESPOONS OLIVE OIL

2 LARGE GARLIC CLOVES, FINELY
CHOPPED

3 TABLESPOONS CHOPPED FRESH
PARSLEY

450 G/1 LB UNCOOKED PRAWNS,
SHELLED AND DEVEINED AND
CUT INTO 3 OR 4 PIECES

125 G/4 OZ SCALLOPS, HALVED OR
QUARTERED IF LARGE

SALT AND FRESHLY GROUND PEPPER

125 ML/4 FL OZ DRY WHITE WINE

1.5 LITRES/2½ PINTS CHICKEN OR
FISH STOCK (PAGE 30)

3 TABLESPOONS UNSALTED BUTTER

1 ONION, FINELY CHOPPED

400 G/14 OZ MEDIUM-GRAIN RICE

SERVES 6

In a saucepan, heat 2 tablespoons of the oil with the garlic and 2 tablespoons of the parsley over medium heat. Cook until the garlic begins to colour slightly.

Add the prawns, scallops, salt and pepper. Cook until the prawns turn pink, about 2 minutes. Add the wine and bring to a simmer.

With a slotted spoon, remove the seafood and set aside. Pour the stock into the pan and heat it to just below simmering point.

In a large saucepan, melt 2 tablespoons of the butter with the remaining oil, add the onion and cook until golden.

Add the rice and stir for 2 minutes. Add the hot stock, 125 ml/4 fl oz at a time, stirring constantly and making sure the liquid has been absorbed before adding more. After about 10 minutes, stir in salt and pepper to taste. If more liquid is required, use hot water. When the rice is just tender, stir in the seafood and heat through. Remove from the heat and stir in the remaining butter and parsley. Serve at once.

RISOTTO WITH FENNEL

450 G/1 LB FENNEL (1 LARGE
  BULB)
1.5 LITRES/2½ PINTS CHICKEN
  STOCK (PAGE 30)
2 TABLESPOONS UNSALTED BUTTER
2 TABLESPOONS OLIVE OIL
3–4 SPRING ONIONS, FINELY
  CHOPPED
400 G/14 OZ MEDIUM-GRAIN RICE
SALT AND FRESHLY GROUND PEPPER
125 G/4 OZ PARMESAN CHEESE,
  GRATED

SERVES 4–6

Trim off the dark green feathery
leaves of the fennel and trim the
stalks down to the rounded bulb.
Cut a slice off the stem end and
pare off any bruises on the outer
leaves. Cut the fennel into quarters
lengthways, then into thin slices.

Heat the stock to just below
simmering point.

In a large saucepan, melt 1
tablespoon of the butter with the
oil over medium-low heat. Add the
spring onions and cook until
tender, about 3 minutes. Add the
fennel and cook for 10 minutes,
stirring occasionally.

Add the rice and stir for 2
minutes. Add the hot stock, 125
ml/4 fl oz at a time, stirring
constantly and making sure the
liquid has been absorbed before
adding more. After about 10
minutes, stir in salt and pepper to
taste. If more liquid is required, use
hot water. The risotto is done
when the rice grains are tender, yet
still firm to the bite.

Remove the pan from the heat
and stir in the remaining butter
and the cheese. Serve at once.

GOLDEN CARROT RISOTTO
with vegetable confetti

1.5 LITRES/2½ PINTS CHICKEN
STOCK (PAGE 30)
3 TABLESPOONS UNSALTED BUTTER
1 TABLESPOON OLIVE OIL
1 ONION, FINELY CHOPPED
400 G/14 OZ MEDIUM-GRAIN RICE
6–8 CARROTS, SLICED
SALT AND FRESHLY GROUND BLACK
PEPPER
85 G/3 OZ SHELLED FRESH OR
FROZEN PEAS
1 SMALL RED PEPPER, FINELY DICED
1 COURGETTE, FINELY DICED
2 TABLESPOONS CHOPPED FRESH
BASIL
50 G/2 OZ PARMESAN CHEESE,
GRATED

SERVES 4–6

Heat the stock to just below simmering point.

In a large saucepan, melt 2 tablespoons of the butter with the oil over medium heat. Add the onion and cook until tender, about 5 minutes.

Add the rice and stir for 2 minutes, until it is coated with the butter. Add the carrots and cook for 1 minute.

Add the hot stock, 125 ml/ 4 fl oz at a time, stirring constantly and making sure the liquid has been absorbed before adding more. After about 10 minutes, stir in salt and pepper to taste. If more liquid is required, use hot water.

After a further 5 minutes, stir in the peas, red pepper and diced courgette. The risotto is done when the rice grains are tender, yet still firm to the bite.

Remove the pan from the heat and stir in the remaining butter and the cheese. Serve at once.

ORANGE RISOTTO

1 ORANGE
1.5 LITRES/2½ PINTS CHICKEN
    STOCK (PAGE 30)
3 TABLESPOONS UNSALTED BUTTER
1 TABLESPOON SUNFLOWER OIL
1 ONION, FINELY CHOPPED
400 G/14 OZ MEDIUM-GRAIN RICE
125 ML/4 FL OZ DRY WHITE WINE
SALT AND FRESHLY GROUND PEPPER
½ TEASPOON GRATED LEMON ZEST
85 G/3 OZ PARMESAN CHEESE,
    GRATED

SERVES 4–6

Scrub the orange and dry it well. Grate the zest, being careful not to remove any of the white pith; you should have about 1 teaspoon of zest. Cut the orange in half and squeeze the juice; there should be about 125 ml/4 fl oz.

Heat the stock to just below simmering point.

In a large saucepan, melt 1 tablespoon of the butter with the oil over medium-low heat. Add the onion and cook until tender and golden, about 5 minutes.

Add the rice and stir for 2 minutes. Add the wine and cook, stirring, until it is absorbed.

Stir in the orange juice. Add the hot stock, 125 ml/4 fl oz at a time, stirring constantly and making sure the liquid has been absorbed before adding more. After about 10 minutes, stir in salt and pepper to taste. If more liquid is required, use hot water.

When the rice is tender, yet still firm to the bite, remove from the heat. Stir in the grated orange and lemon zest, the remaining butter and the cheese. Serve at once.

PEAR AND PARMESAN RISOTTO

1.5 LITRES/2½ PINTS CHICKEN
  STOCK (PAGE 30)
3 TABLESPOONS UNSALTED BUTTER
1 TABLESPOON OLIVE OIL
1 ONION, FINELY CHOPPED
400 G/14 OZ MEDIUM-GRAIN RICE
175 ML/6 FL OZ DRY WHITE WINE
2 PEARS, PEELED, CORED AND
  CHOPPED
SALT AND FRESHLY GROUND BLACK
  PEPPER
50 G/2 OZ PARMESAN CHEESE,
  GRATED

SERVES 4–6

Heat the stock to just below
simmering point.

In a large saucepan, melt 2
tablespoons of the butter with the
oil over medium heat. Add the
onion and cook until tender, about
5 minutes.

Add the rice and stir for 2
minutes, until it is heated and
coated with the butter. Add the
wine and cook, stirring, until it is
absorbed. Add the pears and cook
for 1 minute.

Add the hot stock, 125 ml/
4 fl oz at a time, stirring constantly
and making sure the liquid has
been absorbed before adding more.
After about 10 minutes, stir in salt
and pepper to taste. If more liquid
is required, use hot water. The
risotto is done when the rice
grains are tender, yet still firm to
the bite.

Remove the pan from the heat
and stir in the remaining butter
and the cheese. Serve at once.

THE BASICS

TIPS FOR MAKING PERFECT RISOTTO

Use a medium-grain Italian rice such as arborio, carnaroli or vialone nano.

Use homemade chicken, beef, veal, fish or vegetable stock as appropriate. As an alternative, use a good-quality chilled or canned chicken or meat stock. Taste several brands to see which is best. Some commercially made stock is salty, so taste carefully before adding salt. Dilute canned stock with an equal amount of water.

Cook risotto in a heavy-based, wide saucepan that is not too deep, about 25 cm/10 inches in diameter and 10 cm/4 inches deep.

Cooking time is approximately 20 minutes from the first addition of stock, but exact cooking times will vary according to the variety of rice, the flavouring ingredients and the type of pan used. Depending on the variety of rice, you may need to use less or more liquid. Keep a kettle of hot water ready while cooking the risotto; if the stock runs out before the rice is cooked, add hot water instead.

Risotto needs constant stirring – enlist a friend to keep you company and help stir the pot.

Risotto is ready to eat when it is *al dente*, tender yet still firm to the bite. The centre of each grain of rice should be neither chalky and hard, nor soft and mushy. It does not reheat well, so serve it as soon as it is ready.

Risotto should be served in shallow bowls and eaten with a fork. It is served as a separate course – not a side dish. The only exception is Risotto Milanese, which is often served as an accompaniment to Osso Buco.

Leftover risotto can be used to make a Risotto al Salto, crispy rice pancakes. Mix about 500 ml/16 fl oz of risotto (any flavour) with a beaten egg. Melt some butter in a small frying pan. Scoop up about 4 tablespoons of the rice mixture, place it in the pan and flatten slightly. Cook until golden brown and crisp on both sides. Repeat with the remaining rice, to make 8 pancakes. Serve hot.

CHICKEN STOCK

1 LARGE CHICKEN, ABOUT
   2.2 KG/5 LB
900 G/2 LB TURKEY OR CHICKEN
   TRIMMINGS
1 STICK OF CELERY
1 ONION
1 GARLIC CLOVE
1 LARGE CARROT
1 SMALL TOMATO, HALVED
A FEW SPRIGS OF PARSLEY

Put the chicken and trimmings in
a large stockpot and add cold water
to cover by 10 cm/4 inches. Place
the pot over low heat and bring to
a simmer. Let it simmer for about
10 minutes. Skim off the foam that
rises to the surface.

When the foam stops rising, add
the vegetables. Cook over very low
heat for 3–4 hours.

Leave the stock to cool, then
skim off the fat. Strain into small
containers, cover and chill.

To freeze, place the stock in
airtight containers and remove any
remaining fat from the surface. It
keeps well in the freezer for up to
6 months.

For meat stock: instead of the large
chicken, add 1.5 kg/3 lb meaty
beef and veal bones to the pot
along with the chicken trimmings.

THE MASTER CHEFS

SOUPS
ARABELLA BOXER

MEZE, TAPAS AND ANTIPASTI
AGLAIA KREMEZI

PASTA SAUCES
GORDON RAMSAY

RISOTTO
MICHELE SCICOLONE

SALADS
CLARE CONNERY

MEDITERRANEAN
ANTONY WORRALL THOMPSON

VEGETABLES
PAUL GAYLER

LUNCHES
ALASTAIR LITTLE

COOKING FOR TWO
RICHARD OLNEY

FISH
RICK STEIN

CHICKEN
BRUNO LOUBET

SUPPERS
VALENTINA HARRIS

THE MAIN COURSE
ROGER VERGÉ

ROASTS
JANEEN SARLIN

WILD FOOD
ROWLEY LEIGH

PACIFIC
JILL DUPLEIX

CURRIES
PAT CHAPMAN

HOT AND SPICY
PAUL AND JEANNE RANKIN

THAI
JACKI PASSMORE

CHINESE
YAN-KIT SO

VEGETARIAN
KAREN LEE

DESSERTS
MICHEL ROUX

CAKES
CAROLE WALTER

COOKIES
ELINOR KLIVANS

THE MASTER CHEFS

Text © copyright 1996 Michele Scicolone

Michele Scicolone has asserted her right to be
identified as the Author of this Work.

Photographs © copyright 1996 Simon Wheeler

First published in 1996 by
WEIDENFELD & NICOLSON
THE ORION PUBLISHING GROUP
ORION HOUSE
5 UPPER ST MARTIN'S LANE
LONDON WC2H 9EA

British Library Cataloguing-in-Publication data
A catalogue record for this book is available
from the British Library.

ISBN 0 297 83632 3

DESIGNED BY THE SENATE
EDITOR MAGGIE RAMSAY
FOOD STYLIST JOY DAVIES
ASSISTANT KATY HOLDER